Cambridge **Discovery** Education™

▶ **INTERACTIVE READERS**

Series editor: Bob Hastings

MARK YOUR TERRITORY

B1

Brian Sargent

CAMBRIDGE
UNIVERSITY PRESS

⊕DISCOVERY
EDUCATION™

CAMBRIDGE UNIVERSITY PRESS
Cambridge, New York, Melbourne, Madrid, Cape Town,
Singapore, São Paulo, Delhi, Mexico City

Cambridge University Press
32 Avenue of the Americas, New York, NY 10013-2473, USA

www.cambridge.org
Information on this title: www.cambridge.org/9781107658950

First published 2014

Printed in Hong Kong, China, by Golden Cup Printing Company Limited

A catalog record for this publication is available from the British Library.

Library of Congress Cataloging in Publication Data

Sargent, Brian, 1969-
  Mark your territory / Brian Sargent.
    pages cm. -- (Cambridge discovery interactive readers)
  ISBN 978-1-107-65895-0 (pbk. : alk. paper)
  1. Human territoriality--Juvenile literature. 2. English
language--Textbooks for foreign speakers. 3. Readers (Elementary) I.
Title.

  GN491.7.S37 2013
  304.2'3--dc23

                          2013025110

ISBN 978-1-107-65895-0

Additional resources for this publication at www.cambridge.org

Cambridge University Press has no responsibility for the persistence or
accuracy of URLs for external or third-party Internet Web sites referred to in
this publication and does not guarantee that any content on such Web sites is,
or will remain, accurate or appropriate.

Layout services, art direction, book design, and photo research: Q2ABillSMITH GROUP
Editorial services: Hyphen S.A.
Audio production: CityVox, New York
Video production: Q2ABillSMITH GROUP

Contents

Before You Read: Get Ready! 4

CHAPTER 1
What Is Territory? 6

CHAPTER 2
Turf 8

CHAPTER 3
Borders 12

CHAPTER 4
Common Ground 16

CHAPTER 5
Squatting 20

CHAPTER 6
What Would You Do? 24

After You Read 26

Answer Key 28

Glossary

Before You Read:
Get Ready!

People want to own things. Read on to learn more about the strange and surprising ways we try to own places and spaces, both large and small.

Words to Know

Look at the pictures. Then complete the definitions below with the correct words.

asteroid   border   fence

mineral   treaty   tomb

❶ _____ : one of many rocks that circle the Sun

❷ _____ : a written agreement between two countries

❸ _____ : a large stone room where someone is buried

❹ _____ : something natural we get from the ground, like silver or gold

❺ _____ : a line between two countries

❻ _____ : something like a wall between two yards

Read the paragraph. Use the correct form of the highlighted words to complete the sentences below.

The king wanted to expand his territory. He decided to take some land along a river. It was in a great location. He did not want anyone else to claim it, so the king forced his people to defend it. They were able to protect it successfully from the country across the river.

1 The police said that if nobody _____ the money, I can keep it.

2 Using a bank is a good way to _____ your money.

3 When the border moved, one country lost _____ to the other.

4 You shouldn't _____ people to do something they don't want to do.

5 A garden that gets lots of sun is in a good _____.

5

armrest

CHAPTER 1

What Is Territory?

SIZE DOESN'T MATTER WHEN IT COMES TO TERRITORIES.

Imagine you are sitting next to a stranger at a movie theater. There is one armrest between the two of you. Whose armrest is it? Do you **claim** the whole thing? Do you give it to your neighbor? Do you try to share? Or does your elbow fight a small war with the stranger's?

Territories can be small, like the armrest between two chairs. Or they can be far larger, the size of a country or even a planet. Each territory brings the same question: Whose is it?

Sometimes the answer is not very simple. For example, look at the land around the Sabine River in eastern Texas, USA. Before Europeans came to North America, it was the territory of the Tawakoni Indians. In the mid-1800s, the Tawakoni were forced to leave by European settlers,[1] and the land was turned into farms.

[1] **settler:** someone who moves into a new place

In 1960, the owners changed again. The State of Texas claimed the land and turned it into a state park. The river was dammed[2] and the land was flooded[3] to make Lake Tawakoni. But even Texas could not keep all of the land. They lost some of it in 2007. To spiders!

The giant spider web at Lake Tawakoni

One morning, workers at the park found a giant web. It was bigger than two soccer fields. Thousands of spiders had claimed the area as their territory. People came from all over the country to see the amazing web. Several times the web was destroyed by bad weather, but again and again the spiders rebuilt it.

What territories do you claim? Do you own a house or an apartment? Maybe it's a desk in a classroom where you always sit. Or maybe it's a garden with a fence around it to keep animals out. Think about your territory. Is it yours? Would you fight to keep it?

Would you even fight spiders?

[2] **dam:** build a strong wall across a river to stop the flow of water
[3] **flood:** cover with water

Video Quest

When Territories Meet

Watch this video about an unusual animal found on a city basketball court. What animal is it?

The miner was digging for gold.

CHAPTER 2

Turf

HOW DO YOU MARK YOUR TURF?

If you wish to own land in California today, you'll need a lot of money. If you wished to own land there in 1849, you only needed four stakes.[4]

The year 1849 was the beginning of the California Gold Rush. That was when news of Californian gold traveled around the world. Nearly 100,000 people hurried to the area hoping to get rich. If you were one of them, you needed to bring four wooden stakes.

At the time, land in California was free. Miners claimed their territory by placing four stakes in the ground at the corners. This was called "staking a claim." It meant the territory, and all the gold in that territory, belonged to the person who staked it.

[4]**stake:** a strong stick with a pointed end that you push into the ground

The phrase "stake a claim" is still used today. If you stake a claim, you identify something as belonging to you.

In the beginning, there were few laws about land claims. People could make small or large claims, or even stake a claim to many different areas at once. There were even people who came in later and **took over** other miners' claims. These people were called claim jumpers, and were disliked by nearly everyone.

It's easy to see why claim jumpers would be disliked, but who were the real claim jumpers? Before Europeans came to the area, California belonged to Native Americans. Over 50 different tribes[5] lived in that area. When gold was found there, miners came and took the lands away from the Native Americans. Many tribes were forced to move to camps far away from their original land.

[5]**tribe:** a group of people who live together and share the same culture and language

?
UNDERSTAND
Why could California's gold miners be called the original claim jumpers?

9

The word *turf* means "grass," but it is also another name for "territory." Throughout history, people have had different ways to **mark** their turf. They may place a fence around their house or yard. They may draw a line on a map or place a flag in the ground. They may place a name on a parking space or office door. These markers identify their turf.

When people mark their turf, they expect others to respect[6] it, but this does not always happen. During the Gold Rush, people often argued over claims, especially claims with large amounts of gold. Sometimes these arguments turned violent. Arguments over larger territories, such as countries, can turn into wars. Even claiming small turfs can be the start of a bigger fight.

Turf wars can happen over almost anything, even ice cream.

[6]**respect:** see something as important and not do anything against it

Like most places in the world, in New York City, ice cream is a summertime favorite. Ice cream trucks sometimes drive around parts of the city, but more often they simply stay in one place and sell ice cream to the neighborhood children and adults.

Ice cream truck drivers are very serious about their turf and they don't like to share. Stories of drivers getting into fights or damaging[7] each other's trucks are common. New trucks that enter another driver's turf can have their windows broken or tires cut. In one case, a new driver told the police that another driver had pointed a gun at him.

Of course, the reason for ice cream truck turf wars is money. Sharing turf means sharing money. In a New York summer, that may mean losing over a thousand dollars per day.

[7] **damage:** harm or break something

11

CHAPTER 3

Borders

WATCH A SHOW IN CANADA WHILE SITTING IN THE USA!

The Haskell Free Library and Opera House is the pride[8] of Stanstead, Quebec, Canada. The Haskell Free Library and Opera House is also the pride of Derby Line, Vermont, USA. Finished in 1904, the building was built on top of the **border** that separates the two towns and the two countries.

Most of the seats of the Opera House are in the USA. The stage is in Canada. Theatergoers sit in one country and watch a show in another.

[8] **pride:** something or someone that is very important to you

For the library, the entrance is in the USA, but the books are in Canada. A black line across the floor shows visitors when they've stepped from one country to the other.

The location of the Haskell Free Library and Opera House was not a mistake. It was designed[9] to be used by both countries. From above, the towns of Stanstead and Derby Line look like one town. They share many things, including water and emergency services. Each town has a number of roads that begin in one country and end in the other. For years, **residents** of both towns traveled back and forth freely.

In recent years, however, the USA has wanted to make the US–Canada border more secure.[10] They sent more border guards to the area and closed the streets that ran between the two countries. It is now impossible to travel freely between the two towns. Despite this, the library and opera house remain open, though it isn't as easy for residents of both countries to use them.

[9] **design:** plan something in a certain way
[10] **secure:** safe from danger

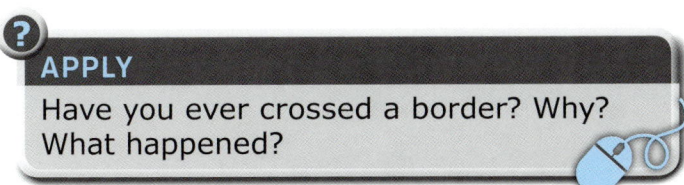

APPLY
Have you ever crossed a border? Why? What happened?

Borders can tell a story. They can show a world that used to be, or a world that someone hopes will come. Look at the map of Carter Lake, Iowa, USA. Does it look unusual to you?

Often borders follow rivers or other bodies of water. In this case, the border between the states of Iowa and Nebraska followed the Missouri River. In 1877, the river changed its course, leaving behind a town that did not know if it belonged to Iowa or Nebraska. The decision wasn't made until 15 years later, when the US Supreme **Court** decided the town of Carter Lake was still in Iowa.

The Missouri River

Both Nebraska and Iowa wanted the town of Carter Lake, but what happens to a place that nobody wants? That is the story of Bir Tawil, Sudan. Or is it Bir Tawil, Egypt?

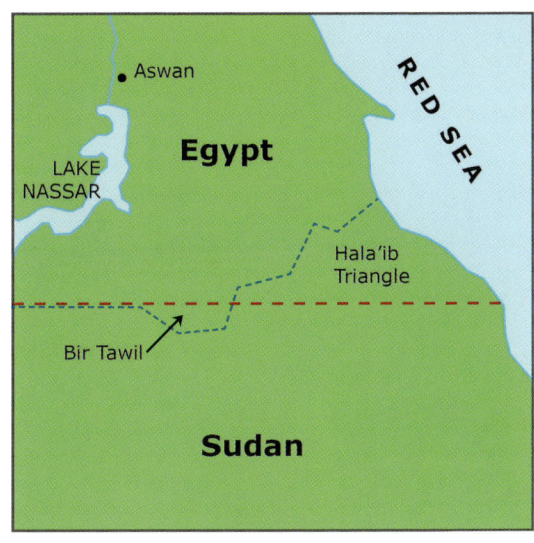

Look at the red line on this map. In 1899, that was the border between Egypt and Sudan. However, just three years later, a new border was drawn. That is shown by the blue line. The difference between the two borders created two separate areas: Bir Tawil and the Hala'ib Triangle. It also created a problem. Both Egypt and Sudan claim the Hala'ib Triangle.

Egypt wants to use the border of 1899, which gives them the Hala'ib Triangle. Sudan prefers the 1902 border. Left out is the small area of Bir Tawil. It's not inside of either country's preferred border. As a result, it's one of the few areas of the world that no country claims.

Video Quest

Drawing the Line

Watch this video about two countries that hold a ceremony every day at their border. Which two countries are they?

An astronaut on the Moon

CHAPTER 4

Common Ground

MOST OF THE WORLD'S TERRITORY IS CLAIMED. WHAT ABOUT TERRITORY IN OUTER SPACE?

On July 20, 1969, two Americans walked on the Moon. They were the first people to ever visit the Moon, and before they left it, they placed an American flag there. What does that flag mean? Does it mean the USA visited? Does it mean the USA owns the Moon? If the USA doesn't own it, who does?

The answer is no one owns the Moon. The 1967 Outer Space **Treaty**, signed by 101 countries, says no country can claim land on the Moon. However, the treaty is not very clear about some things. For example, it does not set rules about resources[11] found on the Moon. If someone finds gold on the Moon and wants to mine it, there are no rules for this. Perhaps someday, like California, the Moon will have a gold rush. Will astronauts stake a claim with four wooden stakes?

[11] **resource:** natural things people take and use

Does it sound unlikely that spaceships full of miners may someday travel to outer space? Right now, more than one company has a plan to do just that. They aren't traveling to the Moon, though. They want to mine asteroids.

Thousands of asteroids pass near Earth every year, and scientists believe those asteroids could be very valuable. Asteroids contain minerals, such as nickel, cobalt, and even platinum. A one-kilometer wide asteroid could hold hundreds of billions of dollars worth of these minerals.

To mine an asteroid, you must take everything you need with you into space: equipment,[12] people, food, and water. In addition, your spaceship needs enough room in it to bring the valuable minerals back to Earth. The plan would cost billions of dollars, but it may make billions more.

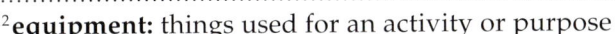

[12]**equipment:** things used for an activity or purpose

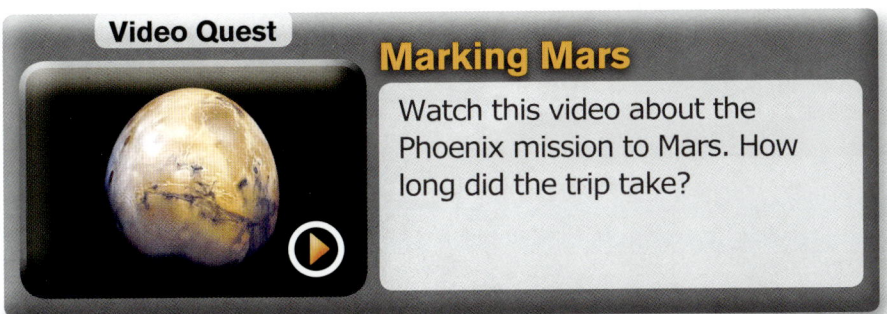

Video Quest

Marking Mars

Watch this video about the Phoenix mission to Mars. How long did the trip take?

The Outer Space Treaty covers the Moon, asteroids, and everything else in outer space. It says that these areas can only be used for peaceful purposes.[13]

There's another territory far closer that is covered by a similar treaty. Sitting at the bottom of the world, Antarctica is protected by the 1961 Antarctic Treaty. The treaty has been signed by 46 countries. It states that Antarctica will be a place of peace and science. It also directs countries to protect the special environment of Antarctica.

There are many countries with bases in Antarctica. All of these countries have signed the Antarctic Treaty and promise to protect the environment there. However, there is a difference between signing a treaty and following the treaty – especially when following the treaty is expensive.

[13] **purpose:** the reason you do something

Russia's Bellinghausen Station, Antarctica

For years, trash and waste[14] were left outside Antarctic bases. By the year 2000, nearly 1,000 tons of trash, waste, and old equipment had collected on the land near Bellinghausen Station, the Russian base. Other bases had similar problems. Australia's Casey Station collected nearly 4,000 tons of waste. Countries were clearly not following the treaty.

Fortunately, many countries including Russia and Australia have now begun cleaning up around their bases. It's an expensive job. The trash must be collected and taken away from Antarctica by ship. The cost for Russia's clean-up will be many millions of US dollars. New Zealand's Scott Base spends 10,000 US dollars every year to bring trash and waste back to New Zealand.

Environmental clean-up shows the difficulties with international treaties. Countries do not always follow the treaties they sign. For now, though, countries are working harder to follow the Antarctic Treaty.

[14] **waste:** things that are not wanted, especially after use

City of the Dead,
outside of Cairo

CHAPTER 5

Squatting

FROM LIVING WITH THE DEAD TO OWNING YOUR OWN COUNTRY, SQUATTING IS A WAY OF LIFE.

Cairo, Egypt, is one of the most crowded cities in the world. People will do almost anything to find a place to live. Some even share their home with the dead.

Outside of Cairo is *el-Arafa*, or the City of the Dead. It is a giant cemetery[15] filled with tombs, some over a thousand years old. And for hundreds of years, living people have made the tombs their home as well.

Nobody knows how many people live in Cairo's City of the Dead. It could be as many as five million. Some live in their own family tombs, sleeping and eating in rooms in which they will be buried. Others have taken over tombs of other families, sometimes earning money as caretakers of the tomb.

[15]**cemetery:** a place where dead people are buried

Life in the City of the Dead isn't easy. There is very little electricity or running water. Many of the tombs are falling apart. The residents are very poor people who would find it difficult to leave or buy a home outside the cemetery. Some families have lived in the tombs for generations.

Most of the people living in *el-Arafa* are **squatters**. Squatters are people who live on land that they do not own. Though squatting is against the law in most areas, it is very common. Squatters choose an area of empty, unused land or an abandoned[16] building. In one famous case, over 2,000 squatters took over the Grande Hotel in Beira, Mozambique, a hotel once called "the pride of Africa."

....

[16]**abandoned:** left behind, no longer used by people

The Grande Hotel today

Not all squatters are poor. At least one is a prince!

During World War II, the British built a number of sea forts[17] in the waters to the east of the United Kingdom. These small forts had large guns to protect parts of the UK from German airplanes. After the war, the forts were mostly forgotten.

In 1967, Roy Bates, a 46-year-old former member of the British Army, took over one of these forts and declared[18] it to be a new country. He called it Sealand, and he was its prince: His Royal Highness Prince Roy of Sealand. The day was his wife's birthday, and he declared her Princess Joan.

[17] **fort:** a strong building used for defense
[18] **declare:** say something publicly or officially

Not long afterward, a group of men tried to take over Sealand. Bates used guns and bombs[19] to stop them. Nobody was killed, but the next year, Bates was brought to a British court for owning and firing a gun. The court, however, decided that Sealand was not part of  the UK, and Bates was free to go. To Bates, the UK had just formally recognized the country of Sealand.

In 1977, while Bates was away, a group of Germans took over Sealand. Bates returned in a helicopter and recaptured the fort. He sent all but one of the men home, forcing a German diplomat[20] to come and ask Bates to free the man. Bates agreed and declared that now Germany had also recognized his country.

Prince Roy died in 2012. Sealand is now ruled by his son, Prince Michael, though the international community still does not recognize the small fort as a country.

[19] **bomb:** a weapon that explodes and damages things
[20] **diplomat:** someone whose job it is to make good relationships between countries

? EVALUATE

Why do you think Roy Bates wanted to have his own country?

CHAPTER 6

What Would You Do?

COULD YOU BE THE NEXT PRINCE ROY?

Sealand has its own money, government, and passports. It is also for sale. Not the whole country, just small parts of it. For around 31 US dollars you can buy 0.1 square meters of Sealand. If that is not enough, for 310 US dollars you can become a count or countess[21] of Sealand.

But why stop there? If Prince Roy could make his own country, why not you? There are no set rules for how to make a country of your own, but a 1933 treaty suggests the following:

[21] **count/countess:** a man/woman in a high social position

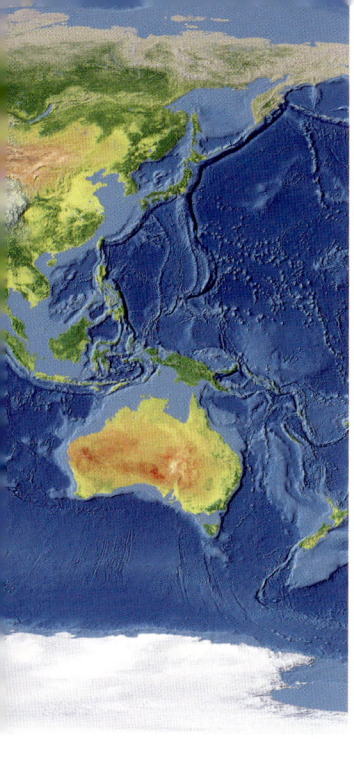

1. You must have a territory.

2. You must have a permanent population. This means someone must always be living in your country.

3. You must have relations with other countries.

4. You must have a government.

The first three are the hardest. Besides Bir Tawil, there are few unclaimed territories in the world. Possibly none. If you do find one, you must have enough people living there that someone is always in your territory. It is possible to live in a country all by yourself, but if you ever leave for any reason then your population has left, too. As for relations with other countries, you cannot control what other countries do.

Perhaps the easiest part is making your own government. If you created your own country, what laws would you write? Would you keep any laws of the country you live in now, or would you change everything? Would your country have a president or a king? What would you call your new country?

Think about your answers and then take out a map. Maybe you'll get lucky!

After You Read

Read the sentences and choose Ⓐ, Ⓑ, or Ⓒ.

1 In 2007, Lake Tawakoni was taken over by _____ .

Ⓐ lakes
Ⓑ farmers
Ⓒ spiders

2 Thousands of people went to California in the 1850s _____ .

Ⓐ to force Native Americans out
Ⓑ to look for gold
Ⓒ to claim farm land

3 The Haskell Free Library and Opera House is unusual because _____ .

Ⓐ it is built on the border between two countries
Ⓑ it is home to more than 1,000 squatters
Ⓒ it was taken over by spiders in 2007

4 Bir Tawil is _____ .

Ⓐ another name for Cairo's City of the Dead
Ⓑ Australia's base in Antarctica
Ⓒ the small unclaimed land between Egypt and Sudan

5 The Antarctic Treaty of 1961 declares that Antarctica can only be used for purposes of _____ .

Ⓐ peace and science
Ⓑ mining and exploration
Ⓒ trash and waste

6 Moving onto land that you do not own is called _____ .

Ⓐ squatting
Ⓑ mining
Ⓒ turfing

True or False?

Read the sentences and choose Ⓐ (True) or Ⓑ (False).

1 To "stake a claim" means to invent a new product.
- Ⓐ True
- Ⓑ False

2 Borders between countries can sometimes change.
- Ⓐ True
- Ⓑ False

3 The Outer Space Treaty covers the Moon, but not other planets.
- Ⓐ True
- Ⓑ False

4 No one knows how many people are living in Cairo's City of the Dead.
- Ⓐ True
- Ⓑ False

Complete the Sentences

Use the words in the box to complete the sentences.

asteroids	border	claimed	declared	treaty	turf

1 In the future, we may mine _____ for minerals.

2 The Outer Space _____ says no country can claim land on the Moon.

3 Ice cream truck drivers in New York City are serious about protecting their _____.

4 The court _____ that the squatters could stay in the abandoned building until someone buys it.

5 The river was the _____ between the two countries.

6 She _____ that the purse I found was hers, but she couldn't tell us what was in it.

Answer Key

Words to Know, page 4

❶ asteroid ❷ treaty ❸ tomb ❹ mineral ❺ border
❻ fence

Words to Know, page 5

❶ claims ❷ protect ❸ territory ❹ force ❺ location

Video Quest, page 7
The unusual animal is a red-tailed hawk.

Understand, page 9
California's gold miners sometimes took land from the Native Americans.

Apply, page 13
Answers will vary.

Video Quest, page 15
India and Pakistan hold a daily border ceremony.

Video Quest, page 17
The trip took nine months.

Evaluate, page 23
Answers will vary.

Choose the Correct Answers, page 26

❶ C ❷ B ❸ A ❹ C ❺ A ❻ A

True or False?, page 27

❶ B ❷ A ❸ B ❹ A

Complete the Sentences, page 27

❶ asteroids ❷ Treaty ❸ turf ❹ declared ❺ border
❻ claimed